THE FALL OF MAN

AN ANSWER TO MR. DARWIN'S

"DESCENT OF MAN,'

BEING

A COMPLETE REFUTATION,

BY COMMON SENSE ARGUMENTS,

OF THE

THEORY OF THE DEVELOPMENT OF THE HUMAN

RACE BY MEANS OF NATURAL SELECTION.

———————

LONDON :

SAMUEL TINSLEY, 10, SOUTHAMPTON ST., STRAND.

1873.

PREFACE.

IT certainly has seemed to me the height of presumption for one, without scientific or literary acquirements, to attempt to refute the theory of so distinguished and universally admired an author as Mr. Darwin—a theory which has met with so much support from clever and enlightened men; and which men, far cleverer and more experienced than myself, though disapproving and disagreeing with it, have not attempted to refute.

It is, however, a well-established fact, that a man, however learned and clever, and however honest his intentions, may be so enraptured with some fond imagination of his mind as to fail to perceive its logical defects; and may, if a clever and gifted author, so ingeniously use his powers as, unintentionally, to gloss over these defects, and that so skilfully as to prevent clearsighted men from observing them; and the logical defects of a theory thus put forward may, by the merest accident, occur for the first time to some person utterly ignorant and inexperienced in comparison with those who have failed to perceive them. I trust, therefore, it will not be considered great presumption on my part to publish this Refutation, and that Mr. Darwin will not feel aggrieved at being taken to task by a tyro, like myself; but will consider it sufficient honour, that having, like many other distinguished men, had the misfortune to espouse an untenable theory, he has by his wonderful literary talent forced its belief on the minds of so many eminent men; and that he will remember the declaration of Our Lord, that God has hidden many things from the wise and prudent, and has revealed them unto babes.

In reading very recently, from mere curiosity,

the 'Descent of Man,' the theory there set forth seemed to me so monstrous, so subversive of all morals, and, above all, so totally opposed to the Bible, that I felt convinced of its complete fallacy, and, on mature reflection, thought that it could be completely refuted by arguments founded on mere common sense and simple reasoning. I confess I was somewhat staggered at the thought that, if this were so, it would long since have been accomplished by men far cleverer than myself; but the more I considered it the more convinced I became that my arguments were well founded and logical, and, if so, then destructive of Mr. Darwin's theory; and from that conviction, and for the reasons stated above, I determined that my ignorance and inexperience should not deter me from placing them before the public; who, I trust, will excuse any faults in composition, and will give me a fair and impartial hearing, which is all that I hope for or desire.

POSTSCRIPT.

———◆———

THE Literary Correspondent of the 'Bazaar,' in the number of that Journal for the 2nd July instant, states that M. Thiers is writing a Refutation of the Theory of Natural Selection, and is being coached for the purpose in geology, astronomy, and natural philosophy. He may well consider an attempt made in this manner as likely to be futile; for it is not to be expected that a little coaching will render M. Thiers equal to a scientific discussion with Mr. Darwin: it is only by bringing common sense to our aid that we can hope to refute the Darwinian theory.

July 9th.

THE FALL OF MAN.

THAT the Theory of Natural Selection is totally
and irredeemably at variance with the Revelations of the Scriptures, no one will have
the least hesitation in admitting; and perhaps
the most salient feature of that variance is
suggested by the title of this pamphlet; for,
whereas the Bible plainly declares that man
was created with a more perfect nature than
he at present possesses, and that he has fallen
from a nobler state to his present position, the
theory of natural selection represents him as
at present enjoying the highest state of perfection as yet attained by him, and as having
risen thereto from a lower state of being.

It is my object to vindicate the truth of the
Bible from this attack: firstly, by proving

the theory of natural selection to be improbable, impossible, and absurd; and, secondly,
by showing that the Biblical account of the
Creation is wonderfully borne out by the existing state of the earth and its inhabitants.

I assume that the reader has perused 'The
Descent of Man' — he need not have studied
it, or even read it carefully : the most cursory
perusal would be sufficient to enable him to
follow the arguments which I shall adduce in
opposition to the theory there set forth.   But,
before doing so, I would ask the reader to
consider the theory of natural selection when
shorn of the eloquence and ingenious colourings
with which it is presented by Mr. Darwin.

Is there one man who, in his inmost heart,
thoroughly believes in the theory,—who believes
that, by mere accidental abnormal developments, all the infinite and beautiful varieties of
life—fishes, birds, insects, and quadrupeds—
have arisen from one lowly organized ancestor;
and that man has arisen from an animal which,
in its most perfect state, is nearly as highly
organized as a tadpole ?

And yet thus far does Mr. Darwin plainly
attempt to trace back the line of our descent.

But of course he does not stop here. Grant his theory, and it necessarily follows that every living creature is descended from the first lowest form of *vegetable* life which appeared (how, Mr. Darwin does not tell us) on this earth: for the links between the lowest and the highest form of vegetable life, and between the latter and animal life, are just as close as they are between the different orders of animals. If, then, one of these links is allowed to have been produced by a separate act of creation, there can be no possible reason why all should not have been similarly produced; and thus the whole theory of natural selection, which professes to be the only reasonable explanation of these closely connected links, would fall to the ground.

What a disagreeable thought it must be to believers in Mr. Darwin, that our ancestors were apes, and that, by a series of reversions, our descendants may one day become apes! What an astounding and perplexing thought that we are descended from vegetables!

Surely to people who believe all this, either from their own personal conviction or from a blind faith in Mr. Darwin, I shall be doing a service by showing that there is no proof of the theory ; that, whilst almost the only proof which Mr. Darwin claims to have established for it is its great probability, it is, in reality, as improbable a theory as ever sprang from the brain of man.

It has been frequently observed, that it is easier to disprove a theory than to establish it ; and I think all who have read the following pages will admit that the observation is very applicable to the present case ; and I cannot help feeling surprise that Mr. Darwin's theory has so long remained almost unattacked, so clearly and satisfactorily do I hope to demolish it in these few pages. But let me again pause for a moment, to attempt to show how it may have arisen that so many people have been deceived by a theory so palpably false as I hope to show this to be.

Undoubtedly it is a proof of Mr. Darwin's genius, that he has forced the belief in such an astounding theory upon so many unwilling minds. His 'Descent of Man' is certainly a model of ingenuity. Its author spends so much time in proving, by numerous instances, facts which cannot now be denied, and in

proving which he has done good service to
science ; so cleverly does he from the first lead
up to, and almost assume, the astounding
theory which it is the object of his work to
prove ; and so briefly and confidently does
he sum up the result of his arguments, that
probably many persons are, without knowing
it, convinced that if they can accept his facts
as proved, the theory follows as a matter of
course. Do not any of my readers, on thinking
the matter over, feel bound to confess that such
may have been the case with them ? But
allowing the facts which Mr. Darwin proves,
namely, that an individual of a species may be
endowed with some peculiarity which makes
him superior to his fellows, and that this peculiarity may be transmitted to his offspring,—let
us see whether the theory of natural selection
follows so easily as it is made to appear to do
in the ' Descent of Man.'

And here let us again remark, once for all,
—and it is important to bear this in mind,
that Mr. Darwin's theory is based solely upon
the supposition that it is the *most probable*
explanation of all the facts which can be ascer-
tained in relation to the problem.

Let us, then, suppose an individual of the prevalent type at some stage (it matters not what) of the upward progress to be endowed with some peculiarity of mind or body which brings it a step nearer to the human species; and that this peculiarity is transmitted to its descendants.

But, I ask, how long will this peculiarity continue to be inherited?

Mr. Darwin himself attempts to prove that, at the present day, the human race is frequently subject to abnormal developments through reversion to the structure of their ancestors, at the time when they had attained to the forms of dogs and apes. But if at the distance of millions of years—for Mr. Darwin does not stick at periods — the law of reversion still exercises so much influence, how infinitely stronger must have been the propensity to revert to the form of ancestors distant only a few generations! Thus, with Mr. Darwin's own weapons—by means of an argument which is of the first importance to the establishment of his theory—do we prove the improbability of it.

But, irrespective of Mr. Darwin's own arguments, it is evident, from modern instances, that hereditary peculiarities do die out in the course of a few generations; and through the law of reversion, which undoubtedly does exercise its force after the lapse of several generations, the families subject to them lose their peculiarity, and are no longer to be distinguished from other families.

And is there not every probability that this would have happened in every case in which abnormal developments arose?

But, even supposing that a peculiarity *could* be transmitted by inheritance so long as to form a distinct order of animals, we still have more difficulties to encounter in following out Mr. Darwin's theory.

It is evident that, in the vast majority of cases, the lower animals have been entirely exterminated, since there are so few orders of animals now existing compared with the infinite number of slightly varying forms which must have been produced in the progress of development from the lowest form to the highest; indeed, Mr. Darwin appears to consider this (as it probably would be) a necessary condition of the theory of natural selection.

But does it not appear to every reflecting and impartial person (notwithstanding all the causes so skilfully enumerated by Mr. Darwin which might possibly tend thereto), a most extraordinary and improbable circumstance, that entire orders of animals should, in so many countless instances, have been entirely exterminated by animals but little superior to themselves?

Let us, however, set aside all these improbabilities, and assume that a distinct race *may* be formed by the inheritance of peculiarities; and that circumstances may arise which would render it possible for the principle of natural selection to come into full play; even then we shall find more difficulties to overcome in order to place our belief in the theory.

In the progress of development from the lower orders into mankind it is, upon reflection, evident that there must have been many cases in which the race farthest advanced in the scale would, in the struggle for life, or survival of the fittest (which is Mr. Darwin's description of the practical working of his theory), have been inferior to the race immediately beneath them in the scale; for instance, the anthropomorphous apes are clearly more advanced in the scale than the large carnivora; and yet the intermediate orders must, as clearly, have become more and more inferior in the struggle for life, since, even at the period at which they had attained to the form of apes, their mental powers had not become sufficiently developed to enable them to devise artificial means of overcoming the superior physical force of the orders immediately beneath them in the scale.

Indeed, most of the higher orders of animals below the monkeys would seem to have been better fitted to survive in the struggle for life than the latter, whose very habits of living in trees are sufficient to prove them unable to cope with their less highly organized adversaries; and yet we are asked to believe that these very animals have been developed in accordance with the law of the survival of the fittest!

I think Mr. Darwin plainly admits, in his 'Descent of Man,' that the existing forms of animals represent successive, though widely distant, steps in the upward development, as I have taken for granted in the last argument. He even places many of the existing animals in their probable order of development. But if he should attempt to escape from my last argument in the only way which appears to me possible—namely, by supposing that the ancestors of man have *not* passed through all the existing forms of lower animals, but that some of the latter are offshoots of the great family, having become developed into their present forms in the same way as man, but in a lower degree, from some common ancestor— we fix him in a greater dilemma than before. For, in this case, there must have been several processes of natural selection going on at the same time, and that, too, amongst nearly allied species; which is obviously utterly impossible, because the dominant race would infallibly have exterminated the members of the lower form of development before the members of the higher form immediately beneath themselves.

Thus, even assuming an improbability following on an improbability, and taking into consideration everything which can be urged on the other side, we are still left an argument which shows the utter unreasonableness of the theory of natural selection.

But we have still stronger grounds than

these, if stronger grounds be possible, for dis-
puting Mr. Darwin's theory.

Since, in every case, the orders of animals
immediately beneath the existing races in the
scale have become totally exterminated,—which
is, indeed, in accordance with the principle of
natural selection,—surely we need some explanation of the reason why these existing races
in their turn were not exterminated by the
orders immediately above them. But no such
explanation does Mr. Darwin vouchsafe us; and
for a very good reason—that, as I believe,
no such explanation is possible. I hope, however, to show that these existing forms of
lower animals in themselves furnish us with
a conclusive argument against Mr. Darwin's
theory.

The only way in which animals of a lower
stage of development could escape extermination, in accordance with the principle of natural
selection (unless they were required by the
higher animals for food, which we know that
many of the existing forms could not have been),
would be by taking refuge in some remote or
less fertile region, where they were suffered to
remain unmolested.

We thus arrive at the following extraordinary state of things: namely, that every fertile region of the inhabited earth,—or, in other words, of that portion of the earth to which access could as yet have been obtained from the place in which the first form of life was produced,—would have been populated only by the highest class of animals then existing; and this would have been strictly the case at the time when the herbivora were the highest class of animals; and, during the reign of the carnivora, and even when the human race became developed, only those animals would have been allowed to remain in the fertile regions which were good for food.

Did ever a theory lead to more absurd and impossible consequences?

But this is not all.

Those animals which had taken refuge in remote or less fertile regions, would not long have remained unmolested; for some of their superiors in the scale, whose turn it was to become exterminated, would have been sure to find out these retreats, and would have exterminated those animals which had previously taken refuge there. Thus, supposing that total extermination was not invariably carried out in the process of natural selection, the various animals left surviving, in accordance with that principle, would necessarily be those immediately beneath each other in the scale, which we see is not the case; for, as Mr. Darwin himself admits, there must have been very many orders of creatures between any two existing forms.

We thus prove, by the mere existence of animals which we every day see, the impossibility of the theory of natural selection.

We have, of course, hitherto been speaking only of terrestrial animals. In the case of the inhabitants of the air and the water, where the chances of an order being exterminated are even more remote, the application of the theory of natural selection is obviously still more difficult and more open to proofs of its impossibility.

Probably more arguments of the above kind could be adduced with a little thought, but they would necessarily involve a good deal of repetition, with which I should not wish to trouble the reader, even if I had them ready;

I will, therefore, proceed at once to a fresh view of the subject.

We have a totally independent proof of the falseness of the theory of natural selection in the fact that there are animals precisely like each other at both poles. Take, for instance, seals—and I think I shall be able to show that this fact is more important than it may at first sight appear, and that it would, of itself, be sufficient to refute Mr. Darwin's theory. For, according to this theory, every existing form of life must have become developed from one and the same primeval ancestor; because, as we have before observed, if a separate act of creation is allowed to have taken place at any period, there can be no reason why every variety of life should not have been thus produced. All animals must, therefore, have been dispersed over the earth from some one spot on its surface.

Now, it will be admitted, that no terrestrial animal indigenous to either pole, such as the animal in question, could by any possibility traverse the earth from one pole to the other. We are, therefore, reduced, in order to explain the above fact in accordance with the principle of natural selection, to the following theory.

Different individuals of some order of animals, which must obviously have been very far removed indeed from a seal, must have travelled, as far as it would be possible for individuals of one race to do so, from the equator towards each pole, and have there taken up their abode. In course of time some individuals of these colonies must have become endowed with some peculiarity of construction, which enabled them to penetrate still further towards the poles, and, by the principle of natural selection, have formed a distinct race. This process must have gone on until, after perhaps thousands, certainly a vast number, of these slow developments, seals were at length produced.

Now, is it within the range of possibility, much less of probability, that these races, totally disconnected, should, in the course of thousands of ages, by mere accident, pass through precisely the same abnormal developments, probably thousands in number, and finally produce identically the same animal, as dissimilar from the common ancestor as a man is from a cat? And yet the believer in the theory of natural selection must credit all this.

And I should wish to remind my readers, whilst we are engaged on the subject, that this fact, destructive as it is of Mr. Darwin's theory, is not in the least opposed to the Biblical account of the Creation. There is nothing in that account which would induce us to believe that all animals were created in the same spot; nor could the most rigid believer in the Bible contend that polar animals were created in the Garden of Eden, any more than were marine fishes; and we may observe, that the only animals which God is mentioned to have brought before Adam for him to select a help-meet from them, or to see what he would call them, as the Bible expresses it, were, " beasts of the field and fowl of the air." It is perfectly in accordance with the Biblical account to suppose that every animal was created in a part of the earth adapted to its organization and habits of life.

I have no doubt that other instances of this kind might be brought forward to prove the impossibility of the theory of natural selection · but my desire is to be as brief as possible, since the shorter my proof of the falseness of the theory is, the more easily will it be followed, and the more forcibly will it convince.

I cannot, however, refrain from briefly showing the absurdity of the theory apart from its improbability.

I ask Mr. Darwin to tell us where this process of development by natural selection is to end?

I can see no reason why, if we grant the theory, further development should be impossible. We can imagine that a man who could fly would be fitter to survive in the struggle for life than a man who was not endowed with that faculty: he would be able to travel faster and with less exertion and inconvenience, and would thus have an advantage in commercial and other pursuits; he would escape injuries and death from falling, and from other causes; he would be able to soar to a great height, and behold the wonders of the earth, and, at the same time, its littleness; and thus his knowledge and science would be increased and his mind enlarged. And we cannot say that at the present day the struggle for life is less severe than in former times. Why should not a man, some day, be endowed with rudiments of wings (I do not use the word in the strictly technical sense which Mr. Darwin attaches to it), or even inherit them through reversion; transmit them to his offspring, and these, through continual exercise of their powers of volition, gradually increase them, until, at length, a race of human beings should be developed, who could fly with the ease and velocity of a swift?

Granting the principle of natural selection, I can see no reason why this and similar absurdities should not happen.

It is not my purpose to adduce any arguments in denial of the theory of sexual selection. Mr. Darwin himself acknowledges that the conditions necessary for the working of this theory are far more complex and unlikely to occur than those required for the working of natural selection. I should, therefore, be merely wasting time in refuting it; and if I have disproved the latter theory, I imagine no one would be so bold as to contend the truth of the former; that I *have* done so, I can only hope that the reader is as well satisfied as I am myself.

And now for the second portion of my task.

Mr. Darwin, in his 'Descent of Man,' utterly ignores the Bible and its account of the Creation; but he admits, that amongst every race of human beings there is a belief in the existence of a God. Surely he will not contend that this universal instinct is erroneous? Grant that there is a powerful God; it is enough for my purpose. We know that the earth was at one time uninhabitable by living organisms. As soon as it became in a fit state to support life, God placed on it living organisms, adapted to its then existing condition. These were, of course, the lowest forms of life. As the earth became fit for them, He created new and more perfect creatures, all formed on the same consistent design, graduating, with perfect consistency and harmony, from the lowest vegetable organism to the perfection of all creatures—mankind. Mr. Darwin proves nothing which is in the smallest degree opposed to this old and orthodox view. The fact that abnormal developments in the human race invariably correspond with normal developments in the lower animals,—which is the only fact proved by him which I can call to mind that can appear to any one in the least opposed to the above view,—is really only what we should expect in accordance with that view; seeing that all animals were made on one uniform design, and that man, being the most perfect creature, cannot be more perfect in his structure, which would, therefore, if varying from the normal type, naturally conform to some of the infinite varieties of structure of inferior animals made on the same general plan as himself. Probably any abnormal development not existing in a normal form in any creature would be fatal to life.

Mr. Darwin says it is absurd to suppose that the infinite varieties of life are the results of separate acts of creation: it seems to me, on the contrary, that the belief that such is the case presents us with the most beautiful and harmonious consistency of design and execution which it is possible to conceive.

But all these beautiful and glorious works of God were not created to drag out the degraded and painful existences to which they are now doomed. Had it not been for man's disobedience, the animals inhabiting the earth, which even now show so plainly their capabilities of enjoying the sweets of life, would have been at liberty to do so without let or hindrance. There would have been no sickness, no suffering, no cruelty. The robin would have sung and sported with his mate without fear of the hawk; the ox would have grazed in the peaceful valleys, and have met no untimely end by the butcher's knife; the horse would have roamed over the prairies, happily ignorant of the galling yoke and the cruel spur; man would still have fed on the fruit of the earth, as in the days before his fall, and have had no occasion to toil for his living; the beasts, too, would still have been sustained by fruits and herbs (see Genesis i. 30), instead of preying upon each other; and all animals would have lived peaceably and happily together. Man's high talents would have been exercised in pursuits worthy of their sublime character, instead of being degraded to the pursuit of filthy lucre and the struggle to obtain a bare subsistence; and his soul, that divine gift, the breath of God Himself, instead of, as is now too frequently the case, lying dormant and useless, would have fulfilled its sublime and glorious purpose of communion with God.

It is true that man and beasts would have
died, they would not have inhabited this earth
for ever: the punishment of sin was, *not* death
to the body, but death to the soul; the terrible
and expressive sentence of God was "dying
thou *shalt* die." But death would probably have
been painless; the soul would have passed
away from the body without a struggle, to a
still happier and more glorious state of existence.

Can any one imagine that God created man
and animals to fulfil their present ignominious
and wretched destinies? Is it not the more
rational and the more elevating idea to suppose that He intended man to live on the
earth as the lord of creation, with no cares
for his sustenance or his clothing, and with
all his faculties free to be engaged in ennobling
pursuits, and his soul kept in a fit state for
communion with God and His angels; and
that the lower creation was intended to delight
and expand man's senses of the beautiful and
the sublime, and to afford him means of re-
creation and innocent enjoyment?

And that this intention of God was not
carried out, we have no right to complain.

By an act of which God alone is capable—
that of limiting His own powers—He made
man free to act as he chose, independently of
Himself; and gave him a means of exercising
his self-control by laying a command upon
him, at the same time plainly informing him
of the consequences of disobedience. An angel
could not have broken the command; but man,
being free to control his own movements,
did so. "God is not a man, that he should
repent," says the Scripture. No; and therefore the command being broken, the fore-
doomed consequences must follow. Only by a
sacrifice, of the magnitude of which we can
form no conception, and the means of the
efficacy of which we are incapable of under-
standing, could the sentence of punishment be
mitigated.

It is useless to blame our first father for his
disobedience; we can only thank God for
making that great sacrifice which has saved
us from the full punishment of the sin.

Does not a consideration of these facts, revealed
to us by Scripture, impress the mind with a
conviction of their truth, and lead to true humi-
lity and a conscientious discharge of our duties?

In the present day, when so many clever and ingenious theories are invented which deny and set at nought the sacred revelations of that Book from whose influence have sprung all the social and national blessings which mankind enjoys, it seems to me a good thing to disprove some, at least, of them; and that I might succeed in disposing for ever of the dangerous theory of natural selection, has been my object and my sincere hope in publishing this little work.

THE END.

LONDON :
EDWARD J. FRANCIS, TOOK'S COURT,
CHANCERY LANE, E.C.

www.ingramcontent.com/pod-product-compliance
Lightning Source LLC
Chambersburg PA
CBHW081308040426
42452CB00014B/2700